Take tha

your race

A collection of humorous verse

Other Books by the Author

Thoughts from a Faraway Place, a collection of poetry (2021)
ISBN 978-1-7884824-1-7
Spid the Spider Has a Day Off (2021)
ISBN 978-1-9996698-5-0
Spid the Spider Battles a Pandemic (2021)
ISBN 978-1-9996698-1-2
Spid the Spider Goes to the Moon (Feb 2022)
ISBN 978-1-9996698-7-4
Spid the Spider Visits the Seven Wonders of the World (Mar 2022) ISBN
978-19996698-8-1
Spid the Spider Helps Out at Spidmas (May 2022)
ISBN 978-19996698-4-3
Spid the Spider Gets Spooked at Halloween (Sept 2022)
ISBN 978-1-915376-00-8
Spid the Spider Welcomes in the New Year (Nov 2022)
ISBN 978-1-915376-03-9
Spid the Spider Plans a Birthday Surprise (April 2023)
ISBN 978-1-915376-09-1
Spid the Spider Goes on Holiday (July 2023)
ISBN 978-1-915376-12-1
Spid the Spider Helps Save the Planet (Sept 2023)
ISBN 978-191537-6-06-0
Spid the Spider Joins Sir Francis Duck and His Pirates (July 2024) ISBN
978-1-915376-18-3.
Spid the Spider Investigates a Mystery at Easter (Feb 2024) ISBN 978-
191537-6-15-2
Spid the Spider Meets Hamish McSpid (Nov 2024)
ISBN 978-191537-6-21-3
Don't Forget to Flush, poems that will drive you clean around the bend,
(Dec 2024) ISBN 978-1915376-91-6
Love is in the air, a collection of love poems (Jan 2025)
ISBN978-1-915376-97-8
Spid the Spider Grows a Magic Money Tree (Mar 2025)
ISBN978-1915376-25-1
Life is a Rollercoaster (May 2025) ISBN 978-1-915376-95-4

Albums by the Author

I'm Having Fun, Spid the Spider (2020) 06091158003
The Fun Goes On, Spid the Spider (2021) 0796548139592
For Julia and Ukraine, various artists (2022) 0796548016497
Under Ukrainian Skies, various artists (2023) 0796548618226
Tomorrow Begins Today, various artists (2023) 0781005393365
Fun, Fun, Fun, Spid the Spider (Sept 2024) 0604565870810

Take that smile off your face

A collection of humorous verse

John Eaton

ISBN 978-1-915376-89-3 (Paperback)

ISBN 978-1-915376-90-9 (Epub)

Published by Spidling Productions Ltd, Meadow Court, Minehead Road, Taunton, Somerset, TA2 6NS, England

British Library Cataloguing in Publication Data

A catalogue reference for this book is available from the British Library.

Cover artwork by Julia Vasina

Typeset by Shakspeare Editorial

Printed and bound in Great Britain by Biddles Ltd, King's Lynn, Norfolk

This book is printed on acid-free paper responsibly manufactured from sustainable forestry in which at least two trees are planted for each one used in paper production.

To my wife Sue,
our children
Ross, James, Kiri, Sandy and Charlotte,
and grandchildren
Evaleigh, Wyatt and Paige.
Never take the world too seriously!

CONTENTS

RHYME OR REASON

I couldn't budge it,
so I tried to nudge it.
When I failed,
I tried to fudge it.

It was written down,
so I spilt the ink and smudged it,
just as well, no one judged it,
not that they would begrudge it.

I am not adverse
to a line or two of mirth,
so what could be worse
than one more nonsense verse!!!

CANNA-KINNA-UNDERSTAND

He's got a canopy above his head,
a canna-pee below his bed
and a canna-peas to dunk his bread.

He canna-pee in the night,
then eats a canape when he fancies a bite,
but then he canna-pay when the money gets tight.

He canna-play when he knows he should.
It's a kinna-ploy he understood,
then he canna-pray to make him good.

Has a canna-biscuits with his tea
and smokes some canna-bis to set him free.
It's a kinna-abyss from which he seeks to flee.

He wants to emigrate to Cana-da only
when he eats his Canna-loni,
I guess he is gonna be kinna-lonely.

MR BIRDIE

Mr Birdie in the sky,
what did you see with your tiny eye?
Did you see the little boy,
looking to the stars –
eyes steeped in tears,
like drops of sorrow.
Nothing could pacify him.
Not today, not tomorrow.

When you flew by,
you gave him joy,
like a special toy,
for us both to enjoy.

Thank you, Mr Birdie,
of this you are worthy,
flying to make him happy,
this delightful little chappy,
allowing his tears to clear up,
inspiring him to cheer up.

One day Mr Birdie will return,
not to a boy on my shoulder,
but to a man who remembers you well.
He'll stroll outside with his own child
and they'll watch the birdies glide,

looking to the sky
they'll see you fly by.

Thank you, Mr Birdie.

Mr Birdie

DimINISH

If I do not know anything,
then how come I know that?
They say I should know where and how, why and what,
but they say I know Diddly Squat.

I don't know Diddly Squat,
though I've heard of Ridley Scott,
I have never met that bloke,
with a name like that, I thought it was a joke.

I know nothing at all
Yet I can stand tall
And although you think you're clever,
We will never ever come together.

I am not as dim as people think,
I am not that easy to fool or hoodwink.
Even if they think I am the missing link,
I've been around longer than Indian Ink.

The expectation of my skills
may not satisfy or fulfil,
those who wish to see myself maligned
do not understand the theatre of my mind.

I may be suspect, I may be dim,
I may be considered out on a limb
or break into thought on a cerebral whim,
but don't ask me what I think of him.

I may know little or nothing at all,
out of my head or off the wall,
unable to hit a straight or curved ball,
though I am here for the long haul.

Whether or not I cut the mustard,
and more likely to end up in the custard,
if that's the best that can be mustered,
it's not me that's getting flustered.

DimINISH

I, RON MANN

I, Ron Mann,
strong as an ox,
sly as a fox,
wears sandals with socks.

I, Ron Mann,
sharp as a blade,
drinks lemonade,
looks cool in shades.

I, Ron Mann,
hard as nails,
eats straw bales,
more slippery than snails.

I, Ron Mann,
tough as old boots,
fought in Beirut,
aftershave, prefers Brut.

I, Ron Mann,
suit of steel,
less than ideal,
finds it hard to kneel.

I, Ron Mann,
fear no one,
ace with a gun,
killer with a pun.

I, Ron Mann,
served in Afghanistan,
crossed mountains in Yucatan,
but try as I can,
I will never be Iron Man.

CONNEXTIONS

I am often humble,
occasionally mumble,
usually fumble,
at times grumble,
whilst eating my apple crumble.

I appear to tumble,
miss words, misspell and jumble,
whilst carrying a bundle,
in my buckle,
so I can gamble,
on a double,
which gets me in trouble,
with the rubble,
for which I am frugal,
whilst walking my poodle,
practising my Cluedo –
well, it's better than Ludo.

I sometimes struggle,
the world is a bubble,
I spend my time in a kerfuffle
by having tea in Brussels,
by flexing my muscles,
in a Brexit scuffle,
which is all of a puzzle,
which I wish they could muzzle.

I stepped in a puddle,
which caused me to struggle
with the mud on my stubble,
which was not so subtle,
so I had to issue a rebuttal
and took the Shuttle
back home to Bootle,
so now I am going to tootle
home...

WHO-DINI?

I don't know what it is about he.
It is something for which he cannot see.
It must be something to deride,
a quality they cannot abide.
Maybe inside, it is phonetically implied,
concealed, important to hide,
then bound to be denied.

Not sure what it is,
not really his biz.
It can't be his 'gee whiz',
or his occasional fizz.
Try to find out from a quiz,
before he approaches the abyss,
with very much to amiss,
yet frequently easy to dismiss.

He is the opposite of what they think,
though everything that makes them blink,
whilst sometimes ponders on the brink.
Protected by armour, chain and link,
lacking the breach of any loose chink,
without a sign of too much drink
and never before landed in the clink.

The thing is, he is everything they say,
and having nothing to display,
he does not hold any sway,
but carries on anyway.
Those fears he troubles to allay
come back and bite him whilst others play,
before re-entering the affray
and fighting on another day.

He is the opposite of what they think,
though everything that makes them blink,
whilst sometimes ponders on the brink.
Protected by armour, chain and link,
lacking the breach of any loose chink,
without a sign of too much drink
and never before landed in the clink.

WHO-DINI?

CHICKEN IN A BASKET

Chicken in a basket, chicken in a basket,
Dribbles grease through the gaps, which is tragic.
And when it leaked on my trouser groin
it created a round oily circle, between the loins.

My equatorial was covered in grease,
where the basket sat on the trouser crease,
over my strides, whilst sat down,
put it like this, if it was water, I would surely drown.

Chicken in a basket, nearly blew my gasket,
when I stood up from the meal, it was drastic!
My suit of polyester plastic
did not look at all fantastic.

I had a new girlfriend in tow
and had to explain discreetly that we should hurriedly go.

She walked out in front
whilst we were mincing our shunt
so I would not bear the brunt
of patrons and other drunks
making remarks about me and my soaking wet 'trunks'.

Like Morecambe and Wise,
we walked in disguise

so as not to advertise
the scented vividity of trouser grease for customers' eyes.

We managed to get back to her place,
there was no mood or ardour to embrace
as I tried to erase
the greasy chicken paste,
much to her distaste.

I don't remember seeing her after that,
not even for an 'I'm very sorry' chat.
There is a moral to this mishap.
If you don't want your girlfriend to give you a slap,
don't consume a basket of chicken and chips on your lap.

Chicken in a basket, nearly blew my gasket,
when I stood up from the meal, it was drastic!
My suit of polyester plastic
did not look at all fantastic.

Chicken in a Basket

PERFECTIC

Just like a Theologist,
there is room in this world for a Neologist;
the maker of words, sometimes absurd,
to explain a view when the message gets blurred
in a format that has to be heard.

Take the word Perfect,
which is in some people's aspect.
There is no conflict
in the word that is picked.
The flawless verb that leads you to respect
whilst others disagree and disrespect.

It is the opposite of Pathetic,
which denies the possible ascetic;
though not specifically poetic,
it is the opposite of frenetic.
Maybe a little anaesthetic,
spiritually Mosaic, specifically prosaic!

Like the Beatles and the Stones,
either side solemnly bemoans,
the lack of musicality of each other's tone.

Some say one is PERFECT,
to the other they call PATHETHIC,
'neither need an emetic',
in the end, they are both 'PERFECTIC'.

BOXCAR WILLIE

Little Willie Burns
used to love big cars
and spent what he earned
buying American brands
(naturally all second-hand)
from his mid-state hinterland.

He bought his cars, named from stars,
one day he will include of them in his memoirs,
such as how he could drive to Moldova
in his Chevy Nova
whilst eating his favourite dessert, Strawberry Pavlova.

Little Wille, Little Willie,
knows a lot about cars,
hangs around in bars,
telling stories from afar.

There were times with Brian,
in his Ford Orion,
when he stayed up all night
to see at first light,
the magical dawn chorus,
in the back of his flashy old Ford Taurus.

He bought a Ford Galaxy,
thought it went like a rocket, but that was a fallacy,
then there was the Ford Comet.

Its V8, 4-speed manual transmission that just made him
cosmic.
So he eyed a Saturn Sky,
which he bought from a rabbi.
Vamoose, that motor could fly!

But that was way back when boys
were boys and men were men.
Now times have changed
and the money became tight,
no more days of big cars and staying up all night.

Little Wille, Little Willie,
knows a lot about cars,
hangs around in bars,
telling stories from afar.

Today Willy drives a mini,
basic, frugal and tinny,
but it's no ignominy.
In the end, it is all so quaintly silly,
so we can no longer shout,
'Big Car, Little Willie!'

Box Car Willie

SUNTANFASTIC

What a great plan to have a suntan
in December to make me look like a real man.
To look bronzed and cool,
I am no fool;
it was for an event,
so for the purchase of fake tan stick I went.

A quick rub on the 'boatrace',
plenty to spread all over the place,
followed by a shave,
carving around like a moulded architrave,
swinging the blade like a tidal wave,
for the fantastic look that then I did crave.

For the Christmas bash was in the cold,
then I was only 21 years old.
I wanted to look suave for the party,
you know: good looking, tanned and hearty.
By the time the tan had set, I was looking like a tube of
Smarties.

My colour was mixed.
Pale, white, like specks and frecks,
brown in bits,
with lily-white strips around the lips.

And at the 'do',
I might have been in the zoo,
as I spent the night in the loo.
To avoid the one-to-one close-up,
willing the ground to swallow me up.

It took weeks to fade,
a complete fool I made,
fake tan, Tarzán, part marzipan,
half-fake tan, half-baked man.
Remember, not only in December,
when you use a Tan Fast Stick,
that the results may not turn out very fan-ta-stic.

PLATETUDES

It's not that you're fat
or anything like that,
but you can conflate
your waistline with the size of your plate.

The size of the food portion
can cause severe body distortion,
feeding your belly's contortion,
continuously growing out of proportion,
though there is a solution.

I can explain
who is to blame
for your ample frame.
It would not be sane
for your size to remain
with that almighty weight gain.

Size does matter.
when you are brought on a platter
loads of food making you fatter.
Like chips with fish (in batter)
and when you wish for someone to flatter,
your chat-up lines begin to scatter...

When you are ogling that pud,
you should really have understood
that when it comes to food,
fried, baked, boiled or barbecued,
have it on a small plate or bowl, even stewed.

Always remember, never be misconstrued,
if you want to be a young-looking dude
or be a patron saint of lost causes like St Jude.
Have a smaller portion and chew your food
on a small plate. To put you in the mood,
sing a song from Holyrood,
'A little bit of what you fancy does you good!'

NO TALENT AT ALL

My surname is Atoll,
like a chain of islands formed of coral.
It doesn't really matter at all.
However, it is a name to recall
and you will find it hard to enthral
when my name is put together, overall.

My middle name is Talon.
I believe my parents couldn't spell Alan,
or perhaps it was because
of the shape of my claws
or that I was a very lost cause.
Listen to the name itself, I cannot be ignored;
when my full name is announced, I will fall on my sword.

My first name is Noel.
At Christmas it may be good for my soul,
but on the whole,
it befits my role
and allows others to laughingly extol
the three-piece name, heinous and foul
whilst I look on, pretending to smile.

Put together,
it's not very clever,
yet it will stay forever.

It's easy to measure,
to laugh at at leisure,
some kind of pleasure?
At times I recall,
such as at the annual Christmas Ball,
that I am introduced and they call
'Let me welcome here
"Noel Talon Atoll".'

THE LEGEND OF DON SAUSAGE

They say he was a super-spy in MOSSAD
until he had an intestinal blockage,
now lives in a run-down cottage,
the legend that is Don Sausage.

Some say he is a legend,
others say he was a leg end.
Until he came to defend
the honour of his best friend

Sat in a bar in Cairo,
signing a cheque with a disposable red BIC biro
was Sausage's long-lost friend, Hiro Spiro,
who followed Sausage to Rio de Janeiro,
Hiro Spiro's a super-hero.

Then a zip in the air, with a flash and a flare,
flew a bullet right past Hiro's ear,
Sausage turned round,
looked straight, up and down,
and then found
a bullet lodged into the ground.

Shot by Ben Germin, his evil adversary,
smoking gun and showing no mercy.
Don declared:
'Did you shoot that bullet to hurt my friend Hiro?'

'Well, if you wanted to know,
I wasn't aiming at my toe,'
Germin smiles at Sausage and said,
'I was aiming for his head,
but I hit the floor instead.'

Don Sausage was enraged,
his anger could not have been caged,
he took out his sword,
the crowd cried out 'Oh Lord
as he went to give Germin a shave.

'You may think you're strong and think you're brave,
but I am going to show you how to behave.'
He circled his sword just like an act of Zorro.
It would be Germin who would feel the sorrow,
and now, not tomorrow.

The sword slid through the air,
Germin groaned with despair
at the sight of his head hurtling towards the ceiling,
he would be rolling and reeling,
no pain, no feeling
whilst he was drinking a cup of Darjeeling.

Germin's head fell to the deck,
what was left on his shoulders was his neck.
Whilst Spiro was still signing the cheque,
he turned to the concierge and with respect said:

'Who shall I make it payable to?
I hope this amount will be correct.'

But it was Germin's own bar,
and it felt a little bizarre
in the old Bazaar in Cairo,
thought Hiro,
but Sausage understood
from bad could come good.

He knew the flea-pit well:
'You can make the cheque out to me,
not just because I set you free.
The money will come in handy.

'As bribery was Germin's modus operandi.
I'll just sip on my bourbon and brandy.
You, Hiro, my friend, can have a glass of 2% shandy
and a nugget of American hot candy.

'I wish to purchase a cottage
the local authority are trying to demolish,
but with a bit of spit and polish,
and using the best of my knowledge
to give me peace and solace,
on the end of the quay,
I think you will agree, that will do for me,
near to Hinkley Point, close to Burnham-on-Sea.'

And that was the last Hiro saw of Sausage,
who settled at home in his dotage,
making thick soup and sausage and pea pottage
in the cottage they wanted to demolish.

Don Sausage

EGYPTOLOGY

A couple arrived from the north,
he was not backward in coming forth,
desperate to get his money's worth.
Then he expressively stated a fact
so amusing, I think I just finally cracked,
the premise was based on mirth,
an imagined scenario, quite impossible on earth.

There is a lot of charm
on a holiday to Sharm.
It is very warm,
much warmer than here at home.

They'd been to the Great Pyramids of Giza,
an outstanding influence for this unusual geezer.
They are the oldest of the Seven Wonders of the World,
with the tombs giving up their secrets, he was beguiled.

He'd never been as far as Italy,
yet provoked his statement so wittily,
'I have only seen pictures of the Leaning Tower of Pisa.'
The more he spoke, the more I needed some anaesthesia;
in fact it was so pathetic,
I didn't need the anaesthetic.

There is a lot of charm
on a holiday to Sharm.
It is very warm,
much warmer than here at home.

In his life, he may not have travelled far,
certainly not to Thebes,
and his excitement was slightly bizarre
like humming a tune and playing a guitar
whilst eating caviar!

In his heart he did believe,
and we were quite relieved
when we sensed that he had perceived:
'That's just like the Egyptian Catacombs,' he decreed,
'We have nothing like this back home in Leeds!!!'

Egyptology

REFRAIN

If things don't change, they will stay the same.
If they stay the same, who's to blame?
If things do change and it's a shame,
be unashamed, un-acclaimed, forget you know my name.

CONES
(What a Load of Bollards)

I think it's spreading
from Swindon to Reading.
A journey to be dreading
and we all know where we are heading?

Some call them cones,
but with motorway DNA, they become clones,
soon will become drones,
propagating in zones.

On forty miles of motorway lanes
cones become conjoined and in chains
whilst motorists' queues remain,
distraught drivers quietly become insane.

Forty miles of cones
and not a worker to bemoan,
except for one alone,
with a mop and bucket and a mobile phone.

One by one he wiped them clean
so that many more motorists can shout and scream,
at forty miles of cones, pristine,
yet not a workman to be seen.

I phoned the cone line to make a fuss,
the response only made me cuss
at an agent who just said thus:
'Thank you for telling us.'

I decided to take a train next time,

a relaxing trip, the weather fine,
I drew the line
when the train, by design,
stopped,
as there were leaves on the line!

KIDOLOGY

Some people have a lot to say and use a lot of words.
Yet, when analysing much of it is absurd,
often leaving others confused and perturbed.

So much is stated,
usually overrated,
intermixed and conflated,
with expressed views dated, inflated and outdated.

Not much that was said
Could not be read
in a red top paper, instead
exulted by a talking head.

It matters not how many words they say,
it is the meaning and thoughts they portray.
Many words are bluster and bluffing,
saying plenty and simply meaning nothing.

SCREW THE TOP

I thought it was me.
Who else would it be?
Who unscrewed the toothpaste,
left the top not replaced?

But it was she,
in all sincerity,
it was my wife.
And all my life
I thought it was me.

Nowadays I check
the toothpaste's neck
and screw the top on tight
and place the toothpaste upright.

MR E

His name is Mr E,
a name steeped in history,
always wins a hollow victory,
a super-sonic-honest hero, no sophistry.

Not always elegant,
earnest, hardworking, intelligent,
articulate, unassuming, despises sycophants,
tucks his shirt in his underpants.

So who is this man
to which I am a fan
more Tin-Man than Tarzan,
Batman with a Kaftan?

Won't give in, won't give out,
never know his whereabouts.
Always quiet, never shouts,
wears his underwear inside out.

Superpower hero, IQ zero,
writes with a pencil, not a Biro,
swashbuckling Zorro, sends messages inspiral,
transmits to the Internet yet never goes viral.

Won't give in, won't give out,
never know his whereabouts.
Always quiet, never shouts,
wears his underwear inside out.

Superpower hero, IQ zero,
writes with a pencil, not a Biro,
swashbuckling Zorro, sends messages inspiral,
transmits to the Internet yet never goes viral.

Slayer of bad, champion of good,
yet so simply misunderstood,
a modern-day Robin Hood;
well, he would be if he could.

So, Mr E, you are at liberty.
No debt, loans, cash on delivery.
To me, you will always be
Mr E, a Mystery.

So who is this man
to which I am a fan
more Tin-Man than Tarzan,
Batman with a Kaftan?

Am I the famous 'Mr E'?

PLEA(D)SE

I thought I would please the boss,
smile at her, but then she got cross,
I cleaned my teeth, but did not floss,
got a cold look that felt more like frost.

I decided to be nice to my wife,
she said, get a life,
not so much a relationship, more like trouble and strife,
you could cut the air with a knife.

I telephoned a friend,
I was at my wits' end,
I needed comfort to make amends,
all that happened was I achieved to offend.

I went to my pastor,
told of my disaster.
He swore at me,
I turned to alabaster
and couldn't get out of there any faster.

I turned to a song,
it helps when things go wrong.
It's not a matter of wealth,
it may or may not affect your stealth,
but it will sure benefit your health.

So 'sing',
'If you can't please anyone, you've got to please yourself!!!'

MR ANGRY

From Bromley to Bangor
without droppin' a clanger.
Let me speak with candour
about your vehement, inveterate anger.
Perhaps you hanker,
in some indignant abusive rancour,
within a split-second slander,
to gerrymander
like a commander,
you uttering, muttering, stuttering ranter!!!

BACONOMICS

For those who do not understand the English language
understand the benefit of the bacon sandwich.
It's better in a roll.
It's a flavour I extol,
bite by bite or stuffed in your mouth as a whole.

Then add an egg
or two, I will beg.
If you refuse, I'll go to Greggs;
after all, there's a reason for using your legs.

You can add a sausage,
though if you're regular, that can cause a blockage,
you will need to add some roughage.
So, you should eat some porridge
and then acknowledge
your skin,
don't let it get stuck on your chin.

Not forgetting the condiment
and avoid the saucy sentiment,
as some like brown and some like red
on a base of a brown or white sliced bread.
Whatever your choice, make sure that it's moist
and maybe have it without sauce, instead.

MY FLAVOURITE

It's the flavour,
crotchet and quaver;
aroma to savour.

I will endeavour,
without being clever,
to have a moment to treasure
the feast of flavour.

YOU F'COFFEE

For those with a love of coffee,
I think I would rather eat a tub of toffee.

It is not just the coffee taste
(the flavour's likened to toxic waste).
It has an afterburn disclosed as bitter
(With the aroma of an old rusty transmitter).

Give me
a cup of tea
and let the clocks chime
whether tea, lemon or lime,
hot or cold (not too hot to hold),
and I will drink that fluid
like a Celtic cultural druid
at any old day and time!

FAMILIAR RING?

Call me a cynic,
maybe I need to be in a clinic,
but then I like to mimic
anything which is not a gimmick.

Call me a fool,
why not be cruel,
but I'm nobody's tool
and won't lose my cool.

Call me a name;
yes, I know your game,
but you will fail with your aim,
I will not be to blame.

Call me a nerd
if that's what you've heard,
but that's a bit absurd,
it's your weasel word.

Call me nothing,
you may be bluffing,
but you may be buffering,
and I will be suffering.

Call me anything,
and I will do the highland fling,
give me a song and I will sing,
as it is better to be called a X@#!!! something
rather than be ignored as a nothing.

INTERPRETATION

They say that I must be mistaken,
when in fact they are totally wrong.
So do not feel forsaken,
I'll be found out before long.

WHERE'S WALLY?

It was a sheer act of folly,
where at his final resting, lay Wally.
Well, goodness gracious, not so jolly,
we mistakenly went AWOL-y.

The cremation was at half past ten,
we knew that, which is why we got there by then.
So many people looking so tearful;
well, would it be likely anyone would be cheerful?

Well, I went to the wrong funeral,
For me, mistakes are not unusual,
getting there would have been do-able,
I made a mistake, that's undisputable.

We sat at the back,
not knowing to whom to chat,
we did not know their faces,
but I thought I'd seen them in other places.

When it was over, we went to Wally's house,
saw his daughter, son and other spouse.
They asked where we had been;
at his service, we were nowhere to be seen.

We suddenly understood way back when,
we should have been there at ten,
I was given the wrong information,
we had gone to the wrong cremation!!!

Wally would have seen the joke,
he was just one of those kinds of folk.
At 88, his last bell chimed,
we think of Wally from time to time.

Well, I went to the wrong funeral,
For me, mistakes are not unusual,
getting there would have been do-able,
I made a mistake, that's undisputable.

Where's Wally

FOOD, GLORIOUS FOOD

I asked would they like something to eat,
they said if they did, they would send me a tweet,
I asked if they wished for something sweet,
they said they were not looking for a treat.

I asked if they would like lunch,
a sandwich or a brunch,
although it was just a hunch,
I suspected they did not want to munch.

I asked if they would like food,
fried, baked, grilled or stewed.
They said they were not in the mood,
to inquire again would have been rude.

I asked if they wanted a meal,
some veal or something to peel,
they said it was no big deal
and they would see how they'd feel.

I asked if they wanted to snack,
some cake, cheese or a flapjack,
they said they would get back.
I was feeling the flack.

I asked them if they wanted a beer,
that is what they wanted to hear,
they all gave out a cheer
and requested snacks to be near.

INTERMISSION

Yes, no, possibly, in bits.
All these responses probably fit
thus as adjectives, all possibly hit –
the right note
keeping us all on our wits.

THE BOSS

There are so many bad ways to be good
and so many good ways to be bad.
When I'm not bad, I'm good;
and when I'm bad, I'm misunderstood.

Don't get cross
when I'm at a bit of a loss.
Some would not give a Betsy Griscom Ross
to run the flagpole and be the boss.

I am the chief,
no worse than a thief,
a bit of a Van Cleef,
for that, I'll be brief.

It's more than a job to manage this mob,
to duck and dive, dib and dob,
not forgetting to memorise the 'thingamabob'.
The boss, thinker, gambler, counsellor and God!

WORK

It's a matter of fact
that my role is more than an act,
and I practise all day
to get my monthly pay.

So when I'm kind,
I think you'll find,
I have the same emotions as others, with added gloss,
though they're a little sharper when I'm cross.

We are all in it together,
whatever the endeavour,
and if we are clever,
we can work here forever.

FANTASIA

Sharp as a razor,
a genius with lasers
till he got tasered.

Works for a glazier,
never been lazier
until he got crazier.

As fast as a rapier,
looks great in gymnasia,
now treated for megalomania.

BOB SCRATCHIT

There was a gentleman from Dulwich
who complained to his doctor about a dull itch.
Doctor asked, 'Do you scratch when you walk?'
I said, 'Only when I talk,
and I've talked all the way from Dulwich to Greenwich!'

FOOD FOR THOUGHT

Don't get uppity
about my cup-of-tea
or rude about my food.
And I am aware
what you think of my hair.

Therefore, I can guarantee
what you think of me.

COMPUTING

When it comes to printers with ink,
you may wish to download a drink,
as the printer itself
when bought off the shelf
will make the contents of your wallet, well, shrink.

When I passed a pink smart fridge,
I asked the price of an ink cartridge.
The replier did post,
'At that price, you're toast!
Not so much riposte, as rip-off.'

Examine the paper,
aka pulped-down trees by the acre,
you can plagiarise your text
to write something very complex,
which all makes you a bit of a faker.

Not to mention your computer,
fed through a gadget called a router.
You can cut and paste,
make errors in haste,
as when it breaks down,
you'll need a trouble-shooter.

THE COMPETITION

'When you cross across a road,
cross across a crossing,'
was my competition ditty
for a road-safety campaign by Mr Whippy.

How I cursed when I didn't come first.
I was first, as I reckoned,
but in fact I came second,
and the prize for this theme
was a year's worth of ice cream.

I won in September,
as I'm sure you'll remember
that when the ice cream man
parks up his van
and lays aside his tune,
he will not see you again until June.

Didn't see him again till then.
Sadly, I never saw my coupons again.
A year's ice cream lost, and I'm to blame;
I'll never enter that competition again, amen.

VEG PLOT

There was an old boy called Reg
who loved his early morn veg.
When I asked, 'Are they good?'
He said, 'Yes, most of them should,
and the rest I'll chuck in the hedge.'

COMMUNICATE

I knew a young lady called Kate,
kind of a love, but more than a mate.
When she mumbled, 'Join my commune, it's Kate,'
I thought she asked me to communicate.

COMMUNICATION

To communicate is more than talk,
like a bird, you can easily squawk,
so don't get uptight
or they will take flight
unless you have eyes of a hawk!

MONEY

Money, money
It's a little bit funny.
I like cash, I'll give it a bash,
There's nothing like a stash.

I'm not cynical,
exacting, clinical,
though occasionally minimal,
a trite subliminal,
and perhaps not too criminal?

You are objective, seeing perspective,
exclusively elective,
mostly electric, often selective,
and mostly effective.

We are a team, together we scheme,
know what I mean,
prosaically clean,
highest esteem,
super-sheen money machine.

You are objective, seeing perspective,
exclusively elective,
mostly electric, often selective,
and mostly effective.

Money, money
It's a little bit funny.
I like cash, I'll give it a bash,
There's nothing like a stash.

Kerching, Kerching, Kerching!!!

'You will never be alone with money.'

Money

MERRY CHRISTMAS

I walked out on a snowy morn
in the season when a child was born.
I ambled over a country hill,
the air was cool, the breeze a chill,
the ground was very icy.
After my roam
and when I got home,
I opened my presents
quite nicely.

BLOWS HIS OWN TRUMPET

There was a man called Donald Trump,
American President, elderly chump.
Don't disagree, he gets the hump.
Some say he's happy, others he's a grump.

Likes to play a-round, of golf, of course,
Talks a lot, gets a little hoarse.
Likes adult film stars (behind the scenes),
Pays to keep them quiet, so it seems.

He has a rounded body, like a half elite,
Not to be confused with an athlete.
Overtly plump, around the rump,
He says he's hard, Stormy says he's limp.

Dissembles like a trooper,
Drops the inevitable profane blooper.
Played golf with Alice Cooper,
Ducked a bullet from a Republican shooter.

Got re-elected as President,
While setting a precedent,
The first felon in the White House,
Where he is now in residence.

He has hands on the pump,
Will the economy grow or slump?
Will he fall or will he jump.
Just ask slow-witted Forrest Gump.

They say he blows his own trumpet,
but with some help from porn star crumpet
in a hotel room at Lake Tahoe
Is there no depth that he won't plummet?

Four more years in office,
Where he makes his own bed.
He wears a computer and a desk on his head,
So, everyone knows when he's Office Head!!

FOOD AND NUTRITION

I wanted a drink, it was left at the sink.
I wanted to eat, but I couldn't reach.
I wanted to shout, but the intercom was out.
As they explained, the reason they were trained,
was to ensure that no one complained.

A VALENTINE'S OFFER

She said we should wed.
'It's a Leap Year,' she said.
And it's my choice,
a day to rejoice.

I said I would marry,
but I'm not in a hurry –
there is no need to scurry,
ask me in four years instead, I said.

THE SAFE

'It's out of stock,' I heard them say.
Just my luck.
'But you promised it would be here today.'
It was Monday when I placed the order.
'You would know, you recorded the order.
You had my pin, I put my order in.'

'I'm very sorry, sir, there's been an omission,
as I was the staff involved
and the matter is unresolved,
I will not get my commission.'
'But what about my goods?
My needs on Monday you understood.'

'We're retraining our staff, sir,
things will be better by half, sir.
Sorry for the delay,
the safe will be here on Saturday.'
'But Saturday's too late,'
I said to berate, 'I'll buy it online.
For your sale, I decline.'

With best wishes to Office Supplies of Taunton

OWED TO THE BARD
(Or 'A Midsummer Night's Dream' in 9 lines)

Midsummer day, Shakespeare play,
and Puck is Jester to the Fairy King,
the story is wonky,
the weavers,
a half-donkey
and love is the heartening thing.
But in the end, we discuss, the tale proves as thus,
falling in love makes
'a fool out of all of us'.

RISKS

I was a taker of risk
before falling off a ladder
and breaking a disc.
Nowadays, I'm someone averse to a caper,
unless it's written down and signed on paper.

MEDICATION

There must be dedication
to take or administer medication,
do not make a mistake
whilst trying to keep people awake
by giving them night sedation.

LUCIDITY

I forget to remember,
or is it the other way round?
The other day I lost my way,
it was lucky I was found.

SMART

You're so smart,
full of heart,
right from the start,
the full 'á la carte'.

As a meal,
how do you feel,
full of zeal
or a little bit ill?

It's food for thought
that smart can mean naught,
if being too clever
means you're never able to deliver
by pushing the boat downriver,
to another date,
by river freight
to make you wait.

Being too smart by half
puts you in danger of making a gaff,
even when you are trying to choreograph,
you may end up with writing 'a chump' on your epitaph.

Smart is not necessarily clever,
but 'never say never'

does not mean forever,
with some hard work and endeavour,
with absorbing the pressure,
in the end,
we can comprehend,
that
being smart can bring plans together.

WORLD CUP WILLIE

Canada, Mexico, and the United States.
Twenty-twenty six, old mate,
First time in North America since 1994,
Unless there is a civil war.

It's in the right place,
Where money slaps you in the face,
And big bucks are the score,
Even in a nil-nil draw.

Don't worry. I won't be going,
I've got better things to do,
than watching men running after a ball,
trying to knock a ball into a goal.

Millionaires kicking millionaires,
What's that about?
Swearing at each other and fighting,
Endless fouls and incitement.

Ninety minutes of pain,
Before the ref ends the game,
Unless there is extra time,
Until the ref's whistle crime.

Then the penalty kicks begin,
Kick the stationary ball in the goal.
If it goes in, you're the hero,
Miss, and your standing goes to zero.

Doesn't matter, we're not going to win,
We're all hype and cheery grin,
With a football song to help on the day.
Until we get beaten and we're on our way ... home.

THE LIQUOR AND THE BUN

Just one more, then I'm done,
said the liquor to the cream bun,
it's been a great time and great fun,
but I feel like I'm flagging,
so I'll go on the wagon.

Just one more, then I'm done,
said the bun to the liquor,
you know when I've eaten it,
I will get over the urge even quicker,
in terms of life, it is a flicker.

Don't you fool yourself
you're damaging your good health
it is only a matter of time
to hear the church bells chime.

I'll just have one more,
you know the score,
another one won't hurt, I'm still alert.
Oh, what a hand I've been dealt,
now it's affecting my good health.

Times have been great, the more I ate
and the more I drank
brought me closer to the brink,

I know that I have to choose
what I've got now and what I lose.

The drink said to the bun,
'You're not kidding anyone.
Your health is shot,
you have lost the plot,
and you're heading for God's oven.'

The bun replied,
'About all your lies,
now you can quit and get out of it,
to be honest, your life is shot.'

The drink passed away
way back in the day,
and the bun suffered a fatal demise.
So when it was over,
ask why did they bother,
as too much of anything is unwise.

So, don't you fool yourself,
you're damaging your good health.
It is only a matter of time
to hear the church bells chime.

Liquor and Bun

LIFE AT 18

When you are the age you are now,
so much is known,
so much to learn,
the best advice is not a conundrum;
therefore, as a rule of thumb,
it's always best to listen to your mum!

DAWLISH DITTIES
(A TRILOGY OF FOUR)

A FISHY TALE

There was a fine lady from Dawlish
who went out fishing for crawfish,
but when she cast out her line
for a fish dinner to dine,
she hooked in a tin of Brasso Metal polish.

MEAT-FREE MADNESS

There was a young lad from Dawlish
who found he enjoyed onion relish, but it was moreish.
He would often languish
with a cheese and pickle sandwich
and eat it up in a flourish.

SMALL FRY

There was an old man from Dawlish
who spent his life on a trawler to fish,
after he pulled in his net,
he took the fish to the vet,
as they were all on the side of smallish.

PAINT-ON

There was a painter from Dawlish
who started to paint the sea wall-ish.
When he pulled out his brush,
the train did it crush,
and now he runs a local tea stall-ish.

FO9

Along the motorway,
it was dark and misty, with glasses she stared,
vision impaired,
it's cold and crispy,
maybe too much whiskey?

A light shines in the distance.
The message confused and persistent,
her eyesight becomes resistant,
she states with a doctor's mind.
'What is Fo9?'

Fo9 is fine
in your mind
as a thriller, like an MI5 killer,
but this is a blizzard
and it is a hazard,
not to say a bit hard,
to comprehend the motorway notice board.

Fo9 by design
is a Ministry of Transport sign.
The sign is fine, except for the end-line,
it should have been a 'gee' (g)
and it oughta be plain to see,
but the sign by design
showed a nine (9).

When put together,
in inclement weather,
the wind and the smog,
though with vernacular dialogue,
the word should have spelt Fog!

For Dr Charlotte Eaton

MUSHROOM CLOUD

I was never a great with vocals,
my voice reflected my local
vernacular of its time,
probably better that I should mime.

The church provided a choir,
so when short, they decided to hire
my desolate tones
despite all their moans,
their grimaces and their groans.

Each week I would sit on the pew,
singing along, slightly askew,
well, I ask you,
what else I could I do?

They paid me a small fee,
which mattered to me,
and whilst there was somewhere else I would gladly be,
I knew my services were not for free.

Whilst sat on the oaken bench,
I felt a pain in my stomach, bent over, teeth clenched,
I was aware this may be an Elizabethan stench.

From my insides,
the noise ripped along the bench like a joy ride,
shocking the congregation inside.
The sound was so loud,
in another place I'd be proud!
Then the waft hit the crowd,
like a gastronomic mushroom cloud.

I feared there would be silence,
but laughter spread with violence.

The vicar was stunned,
he wanted a refund.

How could anyone in the vestry
let out a smell of an estuary,
I must have been brought up grotesquely,
and I must be set free.

From my insides,
the noise ripped along the bench like a joy ride
shocking the congregation inside.
The sound was so loud,
in another place I'd be proud!
Then the waft hit the crowd,
like a gastronomic mushroom cloud.

Of course, I never returned.
If I had, I would have been spurned
not so much a guff, more of a gaff,
though it made the religious community laugh.

Oh, I feel so much better.

My sincere apologies to St Luke's Church, Countess Wear, Exeter

Mushroom Cloud

MO VIES

Maurice Vies, here he lies
after a lifetime on the silver screen,
though mainly unseen
by film buffs, but it was enough
for Maurice.

From Garbo to Gump,
no one could gazump
his skills in a stunt
without a sprain or a bump,
never ending up a chump.

Mo Vies, Mo Vies,
Had more talent than anyone alive,
If he drank a bit less,
He would have been the best,
a country mile ahead of the rest.

In "Wild Orchids" he revelled
as a heartless devil
when he ushered the words,
which led to the absurd
remark from Garbo,
who moaned
'I vant to be alone'.

A lifetime away in "Forrest Gump"
he was heard to say this whilst drunk,
on seeing the star race,
with that knowing look upon his face,
not wanting to be outdone,
shouted 'Run, Forrest, run'.

If only he had a shotgun.
After nearly 70 years,
Mo (as he was known)
was never really shown
his talents were used, skillset abused,
he remained drunk and obtuse.

Nevertheless,
I like to think of him at his best
when I could go to the flicks
and learn some movie tricks,
not from a crop of current smoothies
but from Mo Vies at the movies.

Mo Vies

(KFC) KAN'T FIND THE CHICKEN

I went to my local Kentucky,
the evening was young, I was feeling plucky,
I was looking for an item on the menu
from my favourite local fried-chicken venue.

I tried to order a K105 meal
as part of a meal deal
but was told I was too old.
I wanted the chicken nuggets
with fries and in a bucket,
diet cola, crisps with a dip,
with tomato sauce dripping from my lips.

I should have had my eyes checked,
or just put on my specs,
a K105 Meal is actually KIDS' Meal,
just how stupid must a man be made to feel.

VINO PLONKO LIGHT

Drinking wine
picked from hanging grapes off the vine,
acid, putrid and bitter
(though in time the taste got better).
Mateus Rose was the brand
in the '70s' hinterland.

After the contents were downed,
a recycled use for the bottle was found.

The bottle itself,
recycled from the shelf,
with a wire up its rump,
a light bulb up its front,
lampshade for a hat,
focal point for a chat.

Plugged into the National Grid,
it looked a bit naff, God forbid!
(But it did save a couple of quid.)

A CIDER DRINKER'S TALE

The jug was full of cider
(after consuming, contact your local
healthcare provider),
a local brand from Sheppy's
drank on the settee
until the bottle was empty.

So my brain
was emptied again.
My jumper used as a pair of slacks
due to my brain being very relaxed.
The brew was very cheap,
plus it aided comatose sleep.

In the morning my body would shake,
to drink it all was a terrible mistake.
With regret, with great sorrow,
I would drink it all again tomorrow.

CAPTAIN ZERO

Captain Zero, the world doesn't need you,
When it comes to saving us, not a clue,
You can't save us or pull us through,
is it true, that you'll just put us in a stew?

Can't stay on the straight and narrow,
or tell a cucumber from a marrow.
Sings like Hilda, looks like Matilda,
usually off kilter, couldn't fill a coffee filter.

Caped crusader,
criminal invader,
likes to smile,
has had wind for a while.

Avoids confrontation,
yet seeks approbation,
wishes to save the nation,
whilst minimising expectation.

Tries and fails.
goes off the rails,
got no breeze in their sails,
like Richter, goes off the scales.

Captain naught,
one further thought,
go back to your squat
and give someone else the loser's slot.

Captain Zero has gone,
never saved anyone,
couldn't save a paper bag,
thank goodness he's gone,
fly the flag.

ABOUT THE AUTHOR

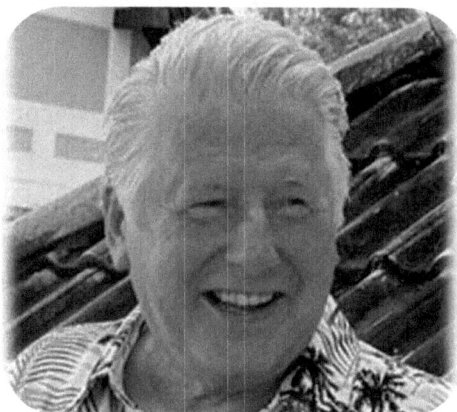

John Eaton is a poet and song writer, also a retired nurse and care home manager. He lives and works in Taunton, Somerset, UK. John has always had an affinity with the English language and is passionate about encouraging literacy and a love of the English language. When John left school, he didn't know what, if anything, he might be good at. As one of eight children growing up on a council estate, he didn't aspire to a higher purpose. However, working in a psychiatric hospital and qualifying as a Mental Health Nurse (RMN), then as a Registered General Nurse (RGN), led him overseas. He went on to establish a successful healthcare training business and, subsequently, a growing care home in Somerset. His work is inspired by the people, punishment, pathos and humorous proclamations he encounters in his day job.

Thus far, John has written four poetry collections and written and produced more than a dozen Spid the Spider books for children. Also, three accompanying albums and many songs supporting the Ukrainian relief effort, including the album, *Under Ukrainian Skies*. The music was mostly composed by Pete Dymond, Dymond Studios. Listen to musical versions of John's work at https://soundcloud.com/john-eaton-205933369 and on all good streaming services.